SCHEDULE YOUR SUCCESS

TOM CORSON-KNOWLES

SCHEDULE
YOUR
SUCCESS

How to Master the One Key Habit that
Will Transform Every Area of Your Life

Get the free Kindle publishing and marketing video training series here:

www.EbookPublishingSchool.com

Published by TCK Publishing

www.TCKPublishing.com

EARNINGS DISCLAIMER

When addressing financial matters in any of our books, sites, videos, newsletters or other content, we've taken every effort to ensure we accurately represent our products and services and their ability to improve your life or grow your business. However, there is no guarantee that you will get any results or earn any money using any of our ideas, tools, strategies or recommendations, and we do not purport any "get rich schemes" in any of our content. Nothing in this book is a promise or guarantee of earnings. Your level of success in attaining similar results is dependent upon a number of factors including your skill, knowledge, ability, dedication, business savvy, network, and financial situation, to name a few. Because these factors differ according to individuals, we cannot and do not guarantee your success, income level, or ability to earn revenue. You alone are responsible for your actions and results in life and business. Any forward-looking statements outlined in this book or on our Sites are simply our opinion and thus are not guarantees or promises for actual performance. It should be clear to you that by law we make no guarantees that you will achieve any results from our ideas or models presented in this book or on our Sites, and we offer no professional legal, medical, psychological or financial advice.

CONTENTS

SCHEDULE YOUR SUCCESS

If you want to be more successful, get more done and achieve higher levels of income, you have to start scheduling your success. If a goal is important enough for you to write down and dream about, it's far too important to just hope you'll find the time to get it done.

Instead, you must invest the time on a consistent, daily basis to do the work that will help you achieve your goals. For most of us, that means we have to schedule these high priority activities into our calendar on a daily basis. Otherwise, other distractions and habits will take over and keep us from achieving what is most important to us.

If you don't actively fill up your daily schedule with your highest priority and most important work, it's going to automatically get filled up with less important work. I can't tell you what that other stuff will be for you, but I can tell you it probably won't be the work you need to do to achieve your most important goals in life. When low priority activities take up too much of your time, you end up feeling like you're just too busy to make real progress.

Success is no accident. You must manage your time effectively if you want to achieve better results. We all have just 24 hours each day to reach our goals.

When you spend most of your time doing tasks that you don't enjoy, or that you're not good at, or that are not leading you where you want to go, your work and life becomes a struggle to succeed. The simple solution is to schedule your most important activities on a daily basis and ensure that you're doing your most important work first and foremost.

Oh sure, you'd love to spend more time with your family and friends, work more on your dream projects and goals, and enjoy more vacations, but you're just too busy. If that sounds like you, this book will help you get your time back. It'll help you identify the low priority activities that are sucking your time and energy and keeping you from achieving the success you desire.

The first step is to create awareness. Your journey to a whole new level of productivity, success and fulfillment is just beginning when you start to realize the way you're currently spending your time won't get you where you want to go.

If you want to change your life, you have to change what you do with your time. And if you want to change what you do, the fastest, easiest, and surest way is to schedule it in your calendar.

CREATING AWARENESS BY IDENTIFYING UNCONSCIOUS HABITS

The first thing you must do to get back control of your time is become aware of your current habits and how you actually spend your time on a daily basis. It's a lot easier to change habits when you understand them, instead of trying to just place brand new habits on top of all your old ones and expecting miraculous change overnight. The world just doesn't work that way.

All great progress happens over an extended period of time. We make a little progress on a daily basis, and that little bit of daily progress snowballs and creates massive change over months and years. The key is to get your snowball rolling in the right direction.

Don't worry; this is not a complicated process. It doesn't take much time. In fact, you'll end up getting more done in less time. You will be able to enjoy more activities outside of work if that's what you're looking for. Making life-changing progress doesn't have to be difficult and painful. All it takes is a little effort and following a simple process that will make your old, unsupportive habits become so obvious to you that they become easier to change. You'll be amazed how much better you'll feel when you finally shine a light on your old, dark habits that have been holding you back from achieving your dreams.

Most of the time, our biggest barriers and blocks to success are the little ones in our blind spot. Just like when you're driving a car and there's a certain area next to or behind your vehicle that you can't see because of your blind spot, in life we have blind spots too. If you want to make massive progress fast, simply look at your blind spots. The problem is that we weren't taught how to do this in school. The old saying "ignorance is bliss" is nonsense! Ignorance is what robs us of our health, prosperity, success and fulfillment.

This book and this process you're about to learn will help you identify your blind spots and make a quantum leap to a much higher level of success.

The key is to start with your daily habits. What you do every day is either leading you toward your dreams or pushing them farther away.

So what are your daily habits?

What *do* you do all day?

The curious thing is, most people don't actually know what they do all day. And I was one of them. That was until I started listening to Jim Rohn's audio programs. In one of his programs, he shared a simple exercise that helped me easily and quickly identify my habits, and it changed my life.

Now I'm going to share it with you.

THE TIME TRACKING EXERCISE FOR IDENTIFYING YOUR HABITS

This is a one-week exercise, so you're going to want to schedule it on your calendar right now!

I highly suggest you start this week-long exercise tomorrow and schedule it in your calendar right now. But if you're really a go-getter, you can grab a notebook and pen and start the Time Tracking Exercise exercise right now.

WHAT YOU'LL NEED:

A notebook and pen with you at all times during the week.

Alternatively, you could use a notepad app in a smartphone or tablet, but personally I prefer a physical notebook and paper to avoid possible distractions from email and other notifications on my smartphone.

HERE'S WHAT TO DO:

Starting from the moment you wake up in the morning (or right now for you go-getters), write down what you do every 15 minutes. For example, when you wake up at 7am, write down:

7am

Then, every 15 minutes write down the time (estimate to the nearest 15 minutes) and what you did for each 15 minute block of time during the day.

Here's an example of what a few hours in the day might look like in your notebook:

7am brush/shower/dress

730 breakfast

745 drive

8-9 emails

9 project A

930 checking facebook and reading the news

10 project B

1015 phone call with John

1030 project B

11 talk with coworkers

11:30 emails

12 lunch

1 phone calls/meeting

TIPS ON GETTING BETTER RESULTS FROM THE TIME TRACKING EXERCISE

1) You don't have to stop *every* 15 minutes. For example, if you're writing a book or working on an intense project, don't bother writing down each 15 minute time chunk until you're done with that project. There's no need to interrupt yourself in the middle of an important project just to write down the time every 15 minutes. When you're done working on a task or activity, that's the time to write down how long you spent on it.

2) You don't have to be *perfect*. If you spent 10 minutes brushing your teeth and 5 minutes putting clothes on, just write "teeth/clothes." Don't worry about timing the small things. That is *not* what this exercise is about. Brushing your teeth sixty seconds faster probably won't change your life very much. This exercise is about finding the *major habits* that are stealing your time and robbing you of the success you want. Some of these harmful habits you might be totally unaware of, and this exercise will help you identify those unconscious habits immediately and eliminate your major blind spots.

3) You don't need a timer. Knowing that you spent 33 minutes and 14 seconds on Facebook isn't any better or more helpful than writing down 30 minutes or 45 minutes. Either way, it's close enough. Let go of the need to be a perfectionist during the Time Tracking Exercise. Major habits will become obvious, regardless of whether you track in 15-minute or 15-second increments. And it takes a lot less work and time to track 15-minute increments.

As Jim Rohn said, "what's not necessary to do is necessary not to do." If you don't need more precise measurements, don't bother taking the time to make more precise measurements. Tracking your time in 15-minute increments is just accurate enough to let you see your major blind spots without taking too much time to measure.

4) This should not take a lot of time. When I first heard about this exercise from Jim Rohn, I thought it would actually waste time, not save me time. I was so wrong! This exercise takes very little time to do when you track your time in 15-minute increments, and I found it *immediately* helped me realize where I was spending too much time on unproductive activities. This exercise helped me identify my bad habits that were keeping me stuck, and it can do the same for you. It also provides a great mental wakeup call that can keep you from wasting too much time on an unproductive habit or activity.

For example, if you have to write down how much time you've spent watching TV every 15 minutes, it creates a lot of opportunities to turn off the TV and go do something else instead. Every 15 minutes, you're creating an awareness checkpoint. During these checkpoints, you'll have a decision: either continue doing what you're doing or stop and do something else. Having these checkpoints can turn a 5-hour TV-watching binge into 30 minutes of TV and four-and-a-half hours of a more fulfilling activity that helps you achieve your personal goals. We all make mistakes, and spend too much time on unproductive tasks. Having awareness checkpoints helps you self-correct and achieve your goals faster.

If you keep saying to yourself, "I should spend more time on this" or "I should stop doing that," you'll find that having these awareness checkpoints creates a structure that helps you take your own advice and make more progress faster, without extra struggle, stress or shame.

5) Keep doing this exercise when you want better results in your life. If you find yourself stuck and not making progress, come back to this exercise because it can help you immediately pinpoint where you're getting stuck by identifying habits that are holding you back. This isn't just an exercise you do once and forget. The more you use the Time Tracking Exercise, the more benefits you'll see.

6) Focus on your own personal goals and dreams, not what society or others think is best. It's important to make sure you're working toward your own goals and dreams in life. As you go through the Time Tracking Exercise and create more awareness and change, just make sure you're doing it for your own reasons. For example, if you try to change yourself to earn more money because you think that's what someone else would want for you, you may end up achieving a goal that's not even yours! Make sure you're aiming for your own personal goals and working on what's most important for you. This exercise is powerful and it will work, so make sure it works to get what you *really* want in life, not what you think others might want for you.

UNDERSTANDING YOUR RESULTS

I'll be honest with you. I didn't do the entire week of this exercise the first time. Not even close.

It only took me three days to realize I had some *seriously bad habits* that were robbing me of my productivity and keeping me stuck.

Here are some of the things I noticed immediately:

> ➢ I was spending too much time on Facebook.
> ➢ I was spending too much time checking emails.
> ➢ I was not spending enough time actually working on my business and personal goals.

Before I started the Time Tracking Exercise, if someone asked me how many hours a week I worked, I would have said 40-60. After the exercise, I realized that, of those 40-60 hours I thought I was working, 25-30 of them were *actually completely unproductive activities* such as surfing the web, checking Facebook, unimportant emails, watching TV, and playing video games.

And out of the actual time I spent working on the business, I found most of it was spent on busy, routine tasks that I could have hired an assistant to do while I focused on the highest payoff activities that would have a much larger effect on my income and personal fulfillment. The more you understand how you actually spend your time, the easier it will be to make the right changes for you.

It's easy to tell someone that if they want to earn more money, they should just work harder, or work more. But when you have a more accurate picture of how you're spending your time, you can start to focus on the small changes that make a BIG difference. That's the kind of leverage that creates breakthrough success.

THE PROOF IS IN THE RESULTS

If you're still skeptical about whether this little exercise is worth doing, let me tell you that it absolutely is! The proof is in the results.

I noticed *immediate* improvements in my productivity and income as a small business owner after implementing the lessons I learned using this simple exercise.

It made my unsupportive, unproductive, and bad habits embarrassingly obvious, and gave me a simple, straightforward, non-techy way to quickly analyze exactly how I was spending my time. Doing this simple time tracking exercise is like taking a shot of pure truth, and will give you immediate feedback on what's not working for you and where you can make the most productive changes in your life.

Imagine your biggest goal or dream right now. Then imagine a role model or someone who has already achieved what you're looking to achieve, or at least something very similar to it. Next, imagine spending an entire day with that person and getting customized advice from them. How much would you pay to get that kind of advice? The good news is that you don't have to pay for it. You can give yourself the best advice possible using the Time Tracking Exercise. What you need to change to get what you want and achieve your goals will become so obvious that you won't need a coach or a mentor to tell you what to do next. You'll know what the next step is for you, and it won't cost you a dime.

You can use this exercise anytime you're ready to make progress and move to a higher level of success. Are mentors and coaches important and valuable? Absolutely! But don't think for a second that you need to find the perfect guru or mentor to show you how to achieve your goals and dreams. You can start to make progress and achieve breakthrough success right now where you are with your own self-awareness and personal knowledge.

Every time I've shared this Time Tracking Exercise with coaching clients, they've experienced huge breakthroughs in personal productivity and effectiveness. The system works. The only question is: will you work the system?

Without actually having this information and knowing exactly how you're spending your time, your biggest opportunities for improvement will remain in your blind spot and elude you. You can read more books, buy more seminars, study from more gurus, hire more coaches, and seek out more mentors, but until you finally start taking your own advice, you'll fall short of your full potential.

As Arthur Ashe said, "Start where you are. Use what you have. Do what you can." You have untapped potential inside you. All you have to do is tap into it, and this exercise will allow you to do that.

Just try it. The worst thing that could happen is that nothing changes. If you hire a coach for $5,000 and nothing happens, you're out $5,000. If you do the Time Tracking Exercise and nothing happens, you haven't lost anything. You have nothing to lose and everything to gain.

I assure you this is what I've found to be the fastest, easiest and simplest way to identify any old habits that are keeping you from achieving your goals and dreams.

Once you've completed the Time Tracking Exercise, it's time to move on to the next step and identify your major habits.

IDENTIFYING YOUR HABITS

Immediately after completing your time tracking exercise, start identifying all your major and minor habits of how you spend your time.

The goal here is to create a master list of your current habits and activities. Everything you wrote down during the time tracking exercise goes on this master list of habits at first, no matter how small or how big.

If you spent 15 minutes checking Twitter, that goes on your list. It doesn't matter how small or big the habit is. Just put it on your list to start.

When you're done identifying all your habits and adding them to your master list, start to take it in. This is how you're currently spending your time. Does it look the way you thought it would? Most people come up with 20 to 50 habits on their first list. A little more or a little less is just fine.

Remember, we were only measuring our time in 15 minute increments so many little things like tying your shoes probably didn't make it on the time tracking exercise anyways, and that's just fine. Some things are too small and insignificant, and you may want to leave such habits off the list. It's not like you're going to suddenly stop tying your shoes because you're spending too much time on it. But, if you spent 15 minutes or more in a single day on something, it's probably important enough to be on the master list, at least for now.

DON'T LET PERFECTIONISM STOP YOU

Don't try to be perfect or "get it just right" when you do these exercises. This is not a contest or competition, and you're a winner here whether you do a little bit or a lot. *And I'm not saying that to be corny or overly optimistic and encouraging.*

What I mean is that there's no "perfect" way to do this. Whether you do the time tracking exercise for 8 hours or 8 weeks, following this process will produce new insights, changes and results for you. Guaranteed. Spending more time on it will often help you get even more results, but don't let that stop you from getting the results you *can* get if you only have a little bit of time to invest in doing this right now. *Every little habit change counts.* Every little change can make a huge difference over time. This principle of how small changes make huge differences overtime is called the Snowball Effect, and we'll cover it in more detail next.

Right now, just realize that you don't have to be perfect when you do this. Following the process works. And the more you follow it, the more it will work for you.

UNDERSTANDING THE SNOWBALL EFFECT

Most people dramatically underestimate the power of small changes to create huge results over time. In the previous example, we used three hours a day of watching TV as a sample habit to change. But many of us may not spend that much time on any one habit. We may have several much smaller habits that are keeping us stuck. That's okay. Even one small habit change of 15 minutes a day can make profoundly impactful changes over one year, five years, 10 years and more. An extra 15 minutes of work a day is equivalent to more than seven eight-hour days of work every year. Imagine how much more you could accomplish with an extra week and a half of work each year. Over forty years, that's more than an entire year's worth of extra work. Imagine how much more you could accomplish with an extra year of work. And all it would take to create that extra time would be to simply eliminate a little 15-minute habit like watching TV or surfing the web.

You can do a lot more in 15 minutes a day than you might expect. Don't let little habits cheat you out of big success.

Little habits snowball in ways that you can't even imagine right now. This is how some people who start working at minimum wage can dramatically increase their income over time. Small, consistent changes eventually lead to huge results over time.

Never underestimate the power of changing a habit, even a small one.

STEP 3

ANALYZING AND FORECASTING YOUR CURRENT HABITS

After you've created awareness in Step 1 and identified your master list of habits in Step 2, it's time to analyze and understand your results so that you can see exactly *what* you've been doing, *how* you've been doing it, *why* you've been doing it, and *where* those activities will take you in the future.

ANALYZING

After the Time Tracking Exercise, we discussed why it's so important to review your results and see which habits you want to change. Right now, we're going to take this personal review of your habits even further.

It's time to analyze each of your habits and get a crystal clear picture of both the pros and the cons of each habit.

Whenever you have a habit, you have that habit because, at some point in your life, that habit served you and provided a very valuable and tangible payoff and benefit for you. Trying to change a habit without understanding this can often simply lead to an endless cycle of addiction, depression, and self-loathing because you *think* you shouldn't be doing something, but you find yourself doing it over, and over again. The reason you keep doing something is because *it provides a benefit or payoff for you in some way, and that payoff fulfills a basic need for you.* Understanding this is a crucial step to making lasting change and avoiding the endless cycle of addiction and self-loathing that many fall prey to.

With your time tracking results in front of you, answer these questions about each major habit:

> ➤ How might this habit serve me? What benefits or rewards do I receive by maintaining this habit?
> ➤ How might this habit harm me? What costs or downsides do I have to face by maintaining this habit?
> ➤ How does this habit help or support other people in my life?
> ➤ How does this habit harm or challenge other people in my life?

Again, whenever you have a habit, you have that habit because, at some point in your life, that habit served you and provided a very valuable and tangible payoff and benefit for you.

The following questions and exercises will help you clearly see both the payoffs and benefits of each of your habits as well as the costs. **This information is pure gold.** *It's the most valuable information you could ever receive in order to improve your life, because self-knowledge and self-awareness is the key to all progress and power in life.*

Whenever you see only the costs or only the payoffs of a particular activity, you will have an imbalanced perspective, and that imbalanced perspective will lead you to make poor long-term decisions. For example, if you see only the payoffs of working long hours, you may become a "workaholic" and sacrifice other important areas of your life in order to fulfill your imbalanced vision of your own life. This is how some people end up working 10, 14, or 16 hours a day and completely destroying their family life, social life, and important relationships. *An imbalanced perspective on life leads to imbalanced activity, and that imbalanced activity can lead to very negative results over time.*

For example, drinking water is good for you. Until you drink too much and get water poisoning (which can be lethal). Too much of a good thing can turn out to be a bad thing.

On the other hand, whenever you see only the costs and downsides of a habit, you will beat yourself up and get stuck in negative self talk and negative emotions every time you engage in that habit, *even though that habit is fulfilling a purpose in your life and providing you with a tangible benefit (which you are not currently seeing and acknowledging).*

According to John DeMartini, whenever you only see the payoffs and benefits of something in life, you will become infatuated with it and put it on a pedestal. Whenever you see only the costs and downsides of something in life, you will become depressed and put it beneath you. Both of these imbalanced perspectives create stress and negative results in your life, and the key to creating better results is to start by creating a more balanced perspective.

ANALYZING YOUR HABITS AND ACHIEVING A BALANCED UNDERSTANDING PERSPECTIVE

With your list of master habits in front of you, answer the following questions and write down any key insights and breakthroughs you have along the way:

- ➢ What would you say are your most productive and important ways you've been spending your time?
- ➢ What are your least productive and unimportant ways you've been spending your time?
- ➢ What habits do you immediately want to change?

> ➢ What habits are acceptable for you right now (you see them as neither very positive nor very negative)?
> ➢ What habits do you love right now and want to keep?

NOTE: It's important to have balance when analyzing and evaluating yourself in this way. You might feel awful about how you've been spending your time, or you might feel proud of how well you're doing. Either way, it's important to have balance. The truth is, we all do "good" things and "bad" things (I use good and bad here as our own personal, subjective inner thoughts and judgments of our own behavior). That's just part of being human.

So make sure you make note of at least three good habits and three bad habits to keep things in perspective if you're feeling overly optimistic or overly depressed about your list. Otherwise, if you only look at your bad habits, you'll feel depressed and negative about yourself. If you only look at your good habits, you'll feel overconfident and proud.

Either way, you're going to be out of balance, and if you maintain that imbalanced perspective, you can end up further self-sabotaging yourself and getting stuck in blame.

Balance is the center path that will take you where you want to go in life. Always try to maintain a balanced perspective.

FORECASTING QUESTIONS

How much time will you spend in your life on this habit given your current daily time spent on it? Add up all those hours, and see how much of your life you're willing to invest in that activity. Three hours a day watching TV doesn't sound so bad, but when you add it up over fourty years, that's equivalent five straight years of watching TV 24/7!

How do you think spending X hours a day [doing your habit] will effect you two years from now? Five years from now? Ten years from now? Twenty years from now? Fifty years from now?

What else could you do with X hours a day?

What could you achieve if you spent that time on your highest priority and most important activities instead?

Can you quantify these results somehow? For example, if you know you earn $50 an hour, how much money would that be if you worked an extra three hours a day instead of watching TV for three hours a day over the next 10 years?

That would be:

> $50 an hour x 3 hours a day x 260 work days a year x 10 years
>
> = $390,000

Therefore, you can calculate that your current habit of watching TV three hours a day is going to cost you $390,000 over the next ten years, assuming you make no improvement in your ability to earn income from working. Over 26 years, that's more than $1 million!

What if you spent every waking moment on this habit? What would your life look like?

I've found this is a powerful mental exercise that can create immediate shifts in your perceptions and beliefs. What if you spent every single waking moment on this habit? What if you spent 16 hours a day watching TV, seven days a week, 365 days a year? What would your life be like? What if you spent 16 hours a day working? What if you spent 16 hours a day doing nothing but checking Facebook?

I know this probably sounds ludicrous. No one would actually do that, right? Right. But that's not the point. The point is that just taking a second to visualize what your life would look like if you lived only that one habit is a powerful way to see both the pros and cons of your habits.

This exercise can help you immediately put things into a balance perspective. For example, you can calculate how much money you would make if you worked 16 hours a day, 7 days a week, 365 days a year. You can visualize that much money and see what it would be like to have that much cash. You can also clearly see the drawbacks of that kind of lifestyle. No family, no friends, no social life, no fun, no hobbies... It would be a miserable life, wouldn't it?

"Money isn't everything" is a common cliché. But the truth is *nothing* is everything. Love isn't everything, nor is health. Are this things important and good?

Absolutely! But they're not everything. We all need a balance of different activities, relationships, habits and experiences in life. Focusing too much on only one aspect of life will always have negative consequences, and this exercise is designed to show them to you so that you don't make big mistakes you'll later regret.

This exercise can help put things in perspective and allow you to see both the benefits and costs of your existing habits.

What if you never spent another second on this habit again for the rest of your life?

This is taking the exact opposite viewpoint. What would your life be like if you just completely stopped watching TV and never turned a TV on again for the rest of your life? How would your life be different? Visualize this until you see both the rewards and costs of living such a lifestyle.

Do the same for every habit on your list like working, spending time with family, key relationships, hobbies, etc.

Really spend time on this until you can see both the benefits and costs of each habit, the good ones and the bad ones (in your own opinion). Start to see the payoffs of your bad habits, and the downsides of your good habits that you may have never acknowledged before.

Who do you admire, or feel positive emotions for who has this habit or expresses a similar habit?

This simple but powerful question will help you see that you're not alone. There are many people whom you admire who express the same or similar habits, and you can learn from this awareness.

Who do you dislike, or feel negative emotions for who has this habit or expresses a similar habit?

Again, this is just giving you even more awareness of the balance of life. You may find yourself angry or upset with someone whom you feel works too much, for example. And yet, simply seeing this may help you see in yourself your own unique expression of working too much or overexpressing a habit at the cost of damaging relationships or other important areas of your life.

LIST OF FORECASTING
QUESTIONS

How much time will you spend in your life on this habit given your current daily time spent on it?

How do you think spending X hours a day [doing your habit] will effect you two years from now? Five years from now? Ten years from now? Twenty years from now? Fifty years from now?

What else could you do with X hours a day?

What could you achieve if you spent that time on your highest priority and most important activities instead?

Can you quantify these results somehow?

What if you spent every waking moment on this habit? What would your life look like?

What if you never spent another second on this habit again for the rest of your life?

Who do you admire, or feel positive emotions for who has this habit or expresses a similar habit?

Who do you dislike, or feel negative emotions for who has this habit or expresses a similar habit?

PRIORITIZING HABITS
TO CHANGE

N ow that you've analyzed and forecasted your routine habits in detail, you already have a much clearer picture of what your habits are and the effects they're having on your life.

Many times, simply identifying, analyzing and forecasting your habits will create an instant shift and help you eliminate a bad habit. Other times, you may need to take it even further before creating real, lasting change.

This is where you're going to prioritize your bad habits in order so that you can choose the most important one to change first, and then continue from there. If you try to change all your habits at once, it can actually end up causing more imbalance, stress, struggle and disappointment. Too much change can be negative and toxic, just like drinking too much water.

Instead, just focus on changing one major habit at a time until you've mastered it, and then move on to the next one. It's far more important to change one habit for life than to change several habits at once and fall back into your old ways shortly after.

Focus is the key to changing habits and making it last.

Now that you've already forecasted your habits and analyzed them, write down your list of bad habits once again on a new sheet of paper. Now, within thirty seconds, choose your #1 most important habit that you want to change right now.

Often, the first habit that comes to mind will be the one to start with. The reason you want to go through this exercise as quickly as possible is so that you don't get stuck double-guessing yourself and lose momentum.

As soon as you've chosen the #1 habit you're going to work on changing first, grab a new sheet of paper and write down the habit at the top.

Next, go back to your Time Tracking Sheet from Step 1, and write down on your new blank sheet of paper all of the days and times you performed that habit.

Here's what it might look like:

HABIT TO CHANGE: WATCHING TV

Monday 5pm-7pm, 9:30pm-10:30pm

Tuesday 5:30pm-7pm, 9:30pm-10:30pm

Etc.

SCHEDULING YOUR HABIT CHANGE

Now that you have all your data in one place from that one habit, it's time to schedule your habit change. Notice when and where you frequently perform that habit. In the example above, notice that watching TV seems to happen between 5pm-7pm and 9:30pm-10:30pm. These are the key times when you must be aware of your habit and have another course of action planned out ahead of time so that you don't repeat your old habits.

Here are the four key ways you can help guarantee habit change at these key times:

SCHEDULE SOMETHING BETTER

Using this method, you will schedule something better and more preferable during your key habit times. Using the example from before, between the hours of 5pm-7pm and 9:30pm-10:30pm, you would schedule something better. In this case, "better" means more enjoyable, entertaining or fun for you personally. This must be something *so much better that you would never think of stopping or quitting in order to engage in your old habit.*

For example, maybe you schedule a professional massage between 5pm-7pm, and from 9:30pm-10:30pm, you plan an intimate date with your spouse.

The key here is to schedule an activity that is so much more enjoyable than the habit that you won't even think about it during those times.

SCHEDULE SOMETHING EXCLUSIVE

Using this method, you'll schedule something that excludes the habit from being a possibility. For example, if you golf from 5pm-7pm, you've excluded that habit because you can't be watching TV and golfing at the same time.

A great way to schedule something exclusive is to just be somewhere else. If you always engage in a habit in one location or place (like at home), make plans to go out and be in a different location where it's just not possible to continue that habit during that time.

ELIMINATE TRIGGERS

Eliminating triggers means eliminating signs or cues that trigger your habitual behavior. For example, you could create a TV stand with a door that closes and close the door throughout the day so that you're not as tempted to sit down and watch TV.

Sometimes simply changing your route or timing can also help eliminate triggers. For example, if you were trying to quit coffee, and your normal route to work in the morning goes by a Starbucks where you always buy coffee, you could simply take a different route to work that doesn't pass that location, thus avoiding the trigger altogether.

CHANGE THE ENVIRONMENT

Using this method, you change the environment so that it no longer supports the old habit. For example, you could cancel your cable subscription or sell your TV. Although this may seem extreme or impossible in your situation, sometimes changing the environment can be the most effective way to guarantee long-term habit change.

For example, many drug addicts find that if they don't change their environment, they can't help but fall back into their old habits of addiction. For serious addictive behavior that you just can't seem to change any other way, try changing the environment. This will often help you change the habit for good.

WHAT ABOUT HABITS WITHOUT SET SCHEDULES?

If you want to change a habit and notice that there is no set schedule for it, it may seem like these strategies won't work for you. Most of them will still work just fine with a few modifications.

The first thing you have to do is find out what might be triggering your habit. In the example above, you could say that the time of day was triggering the habit for watching TV. Many emotions, situations or events could trigger a habit. For example, if you find yourself gorging on ice cream and junk food sporadically, dig deeper and see what might be triggering your behavior.

Oftentimes, it's an emotion or feeling inside that we tend to ignore, downplay or hide from ourselves or others. Many of our bad habits are often just poor strategies for coping with stressful situations and unpleasant emotions.

See if you can identify the exact emotion that tends to trigger your bad habit. Is it anger, frustration, sadness, guilt, shame, or something else? Simply putting a name to the emotion can be a huge step forward in identifying the underlying causes of your habit.

Once you've identified the emotion, begin to notice when that emotion pops up. Are there certain circumstances or situations that tend to cause that emotion to occur? Many people find keeping a journal of their emotional states and reactions can help create more awareness and make change easier as well.

Without creating this kind of awareness, it can be very hard to change the habit. You'll find yourself having already eaten an entire carton of ice cream before you realize that you're feeling awful and made a mistake. The key is to increase your awareness so that you notice the emotions earlier and can stop the habit sooner or prevent it from happening altogether.

Make sure you acknowledge even small improvements in habit change. For example, if you normally binge eat an entire quart of ice cream but this time only eat 3/4ths of the container, that's progress! Any progress should be acknowledged and celebrated. This helps reinforce your new habit change and helps you keep that forward momentum going.

When you notice a habit being triggered by an emotion, see if you can find a more positive, alternative course of action instead of binging on junk food. Maybe talking to a loved one or confidant about your emotions can help diffuse the negative feelings before the bad habit takes over. Some people find that vigorous exercise can help diffuse these negative emotions as well.

In my personal experience with emotionally triggered bad habits, it's not so important what you do when the emotion comes. *The important thing is that you do something different than just going through with your old habit.* Many times being social and hanging around other people can help. Oftentimes, we try to hide and avoid these negative emotions. Rarely do people binge eat with friends. More often, it's a solitary habit. Simply surrounding yourself with friends can help diffuse the habit because you can no longer hide it.

If you have a habit and you're not sure what's triggering it or how to stop it, look to your emotions. See if you can identify the key, underlying emotion that's responsible for triggering your habit. Once you've done that, come up with one or several strategies for taking a different course of action when that emotion comes up that will diffuse the habit and create a new, more productive and fulfilling habit in its place.

STEP 5

IMPROVING EXISTING GOOD HABITS

Most people completely ignore this aspect of habit change and productivity. We think we need to focus only on changing bad habits and not on improving our existing habits. But, many times, the seeds for our greatest successes are already growing in our current good habits, and all we need is to water and nurture those seeds to allow them to bear even more fruit.

As a simple, easy to understand example, let's talk about money. If you already earn $10,000 a year from a habit (like writing, blogging, coaching, etc.), then you most likely have the potential to earn far more than that from that habit. The fact that you can already earn money from a current habit means that you have the potential to increase that amount of income by spending more time working, becoming a more productive worker, creating systems and processes to improve your results, leveraging other people's time, and other productivity strategies.

For example, if your goal is to earn $20,000 and you already have a habit that's earning you $10,000, you can see how simple it would be to produce those results. Simply double your time, or double your productivity, or a combination of both. Of course, that's easier said than done. But, it should be really clear that doubling your results from a habit isn't an impossible task in such a situation.

It can be a little bit harder to see how to go from $10,000 to $100,000 or more, though. And that's where the snowball effect we discussed before comes into play. It probably will *not* be immediately apparent how you can go from $10,000 to $100,000 or even $1,000,000 with that habit. In fact, it might seem downright *impossible.* That's okay!

It's completely normal to feel that way, and you're in the right place. It is possible to improve your results 10x or more. The solution is to start with small changes, continue to measure your results, and make gradual adjustments and improvements along the way.

The Japanese call this process of constant improvement Kaizen. And that's how great things are achieved in life. Consistently making small changes and improvements leads to huge changes in results over time. This is the snowball effect we discussed earlier.

Now, let me be clear. I am NOT saying that it's going to be easy, effortless and that you're guaranteed to increase your income 10x or more if you do this. This isn't about easy, instant, get-rich-quick gimmicks. This is about making small changes that, over time, can lead to huge results. *In fact, making consistent, small changes over time is often the only way to create a huge increase in results.*

But even if you don't see a 10x increase in income, would it be worth it if you could make some small adjustments and improvements and go from $10,000 to $11,000? Would an extra $1,000 be valuable to you? Would it provide enough motivation and inspiration to get you to make even more positive changes in your life?

It can be awesome to think about earning 10x more money or having a 10x better relationship with your family, but often just a small improvement will have a big enough effect to make a serious difference in your life. And those small wins can provide the results and motivation you need to make even more changes, and so the virtuous cycle of Kaizen, constant improvement and small wins, keeps going.

Kaizen and constant improvement don't just apply to earning money, though. It applies to every area of your life – finances, career, relationships, spirituality, emotions, and anything else that's important to you.

It's a lot easier to measure a 10x increase in income than a 10x increase in your happiness or relationship with your parents, and that's why I use income as an example. But realize that these same principles apply to every area of your life. If you made just one additional 5-minute call a week to a loved one or family member or old friend, you'd probably feel more fulfilled in your relationships. It doesn't have to take a huge commitment of time to get a huge return on your investment in every area of your life. The key is to find those high-impact activities or habits that make a big difference without requiring a big investment of time.

FALL IN LOVE WITH THE PROCESS, NOT THE RESULTS

I want to warn you here about a common trap people fall into. Most of us fall in love with the results and end up ignoring the process. We fall in love with the money, or the better relationship, or whatever goals we have, and we tend to forget and minimize the habits, activities and efforts that got us those good results in the first place.

You've probably seen this clearly displayed in some of your relationships in the past. You get into a new relationship, things are going great, and you get into a good groove where everything feels awesome.

Then you start to slip a little bit, unconsciously. Maybe you stop treating the other person as special as you did at first. Maybe you spend a little more time with your friends or watching TV than with your partner. Maybe you stop going out of your way to give them gifts or do kind things for them. And then, you find out they're leaving you because it's "just not like it used to be."

That's what happens when you fall in love with the results (having a good relationship that's going well) and ignore or minimize the habits and activities that led to those results (going out of your way to do kind deeds and show your appreciation for your partner, etc.) When you minimize or ignore these crucial habits, you stop doing them as often or altogether, and you erode the very foundation of the results you have fallen in love with! It's classic example of self-sabotage, and it's a common trap we all fall into at some point in our life.

So how do you avoid this trap? It's all about following this process we're going through in this book (the activity and habits of creating awareness, evaluating and forecasting your current habits.)

By being more aware of your habits, you'll start to see when you slip back into old habits or start to give up on your new, improved habits. Never underestimate the power of self-awareness! It can be the key to unlocking the success you've been looking for.

AVOIDING MAJOR PSYCHOLOGICAL BARRIERS TO LASTING HABIT CHANGE

Humans have two major psychological tendencies that can jeopardize your ability to maintain new habits and continue on your path to success.

First, we tend to get used to things the way they are. If you increase your income by 10x, for example, studies show that it usually doesn't make you 10x happier. In fact, it usually doesn't make you happier at all after a certain income level. Sure, right after you achieve that huge increase in income, you'll feel great. But that feeling soon fades, and you go back to your normal level of happiness. Being 10x richer just becomes normal.

Scientists call this phenomenon the hedonic treadmill, and if you don't understand how it works, it can cause a lot of unnecessary pain and suffering. If you don't understand this phenomenon of human psychology, you'll be under the illusion that having more money or achieving your goal will make you permanently happier. In reality, achieving a goal almost always only produces a short period of increased happiness. After that, you get used to things the way they are, and you go back to your old level of happiness. If you find yourself thinking, "If I could only achieve this goal, then I'll have it made!" then you know you've fallen into this trap. Thinking that you'll be happier in the future is an illusion. The truth is, you'll be most happy during the journey as you grow and learn.

The best way I've found to avoid the trap of the hedonic treadmill is to set goals and habits for myself that are both rewarding in the long-term and the short-term.

People who focus entirely on short-term happiness and success tend to end up unhappy and feel unfulfilled because they haven't achieved more with their life. It turns out that focusing on short-term happiness and emotions doesn't often lead to long-term success. That's why going to parties every night may feel great

FORECASTING YOUR HABITS

Forecasting your habits is one of the most powerful 5-minute mental exercises you can use to create instant motivation for change. This process helps create instant emotional shifts that will free you from old, unsupportive habits, as well as help you acknowledge and appreciate the good habits you already have.

Forecasting can help you see the true costs and benefits of each habit in a larger-than-life, exaggerated way. This can make it a lot easier to see the *real* costs and benefits (especially ones you may have never before acknowledged or appreciated).

Here's how.

Let's take "spending too much time watching TV" as a sample habit, and let's assume you measured yourself spending three hours a day on this habit.

Now, in your mind picture yourself watching TV for three hours a day today, tomorrow, the next day, and day after day for the rest of your life. Can you see how spending that much time on this activity every day for the rest of your life might effect you two years, ten years, twenty years from now?

Forecasting is simply taking your current experiences and projecting them into the future and trying to understand what that future would be like.

Here are some questions to help.

and fun at the time, but after several years you'll begin to realize that you're not making progress in other important areas of your life.

If you've ever felt like you should be more successful than you are now or that you have friends or associates who have "passed you by" financially, spiritually, emotionally or in some other area of life, that's probably because you've been focusing too much on short-term results in that area of your life. The key to long-term success is long-term focus. Sometimes the lower paying job or opportunity is more rewarding long-term. Sometimes breaking off a relationship that you feel has no long-term potential feels awful at first, but can create the space you need to find a better long-term partner.

On the other hand, people who focus entirely on long-term results tend to feel unfulfilled and unhappy because they spend their whole lives working to achieve something that they either never quite achieve, or, when they do achieve it after several years, the happiness fades much more quickly than they imagined. This often leads to regrets. You've probably seen people who spent most of their time working, and years later regret not spending more time with their family or traveling. If you find yourself focusing too much on long-term results, you might want to consider balancing your long-term focus with some short-term goals and fulfilling experiences.

The key for me, personally, has been to focus on both long-term and short-term goals. When I strike that right balance, I find myself moving towards my long-term goals while enjoying the journey a whole lot more.

Oftentimes, a bad habit is simply a subconscious way for us to fulfill short-term or long-term needs that aren't being met. So look at your current balance of short-term and long-term goals and see what needs you might not be meeting right now that your bad habit is filling in for.

WE NEED SOMETHING NEW

A second potential psychological barrier to changing habits is that we crave new experiences. Humans have a need for experiencing new things in life. When things are new, we tend to overvalue them. When things are no longer new, we tend to undervalue them. That's why so many new products say "New!" right on the label or in the advertising. This need to experience new things can create a painful pattern that first creates and then destroys many relationships, businesses, and projects.

Most pop psychology books say that you can create a new habit in 30 days or 60 days, or some similar number. In my experience, it just doesn't work that way. Yes, it usually takes a month or two of discipline to create a new habit. But that doesn't mean you now have that habit for life and never have to think about it again. Many times, I've found myself creating a new habit and sticking with it for a few months, and then, once that habit no longer feels new, I find myself slipping back into old habits again or finding another habit to replace that new one I worked so hard creating.

I'm guessing you've probably had a similar experience before because I've seen the same pattern again and again in myself, with my students and coaching clients, and with friends and family.

A common pattern may be that it takes one or two months to create a habit and start to see some promising results that get you excited and keep you wanting to continue the habit. Then, maybe a few months later, you hit a plateau. Maybe you started the habit of going to the gym and working out to lose weight. So you lose 10 or 15 pounds in the first few months, and then the next few months nothing changes. Your weight is staying the same even though you're working just as hard, if not harder than when you first started. That's when we tend to get discouraged. Why bother working out so much if you're not getting results anymore? And so we quit.

But this is the exact kind of self-sabotage that stops most people from achieving really important goals in life. When I feel like I've hit a plateau in life, I try to focus on my long-term goals and objectives. You might say to yourself, *"I know I'm still working hard at the gym every week and I haven't lost any weight in a few weeks, but I'm going to keep going. I know that if I keep up this level of activity, I'm going to feel great about myself and eventually I'll get to my ideal weight. But even if that doesn't happen, I'll feel better knowing that I'm a person who consistently works out than someone who just gives up when things get hard."*

Again, the key here is awareness. If you find yourself really motivated about a new habit, and then suddenly become unmotivated, check in with your emotions again and see what's going on. If you've already spent a few months creating a new habit, it would be a shame to give up on it now. When you hit a plateau, check back in with your emotions and your goals and recommit to your habit.

This is another reason why going back to the Time Tracking Exercise can be so helpful. Many times, we self-sabotage unconsciously and don't even notice it. But the Time Tracking Exercise never lies. When you measure how much time you're working out at the gym or spending working on an important project, you'll know immediately if you're meeting your goals or not.

This is just another reason why I recommend using the Time Tracking Exercise every three months or so. Usually, that's about the time when a new habit starts to lose steam and we start seeking out something new to take its place. And that's why it's the perfect time to check back in, create more self-awareness, and make sure you're still on the right track.

STEP 6

CREATING MASSIVE RESULTS
BY CHANGING ONE HABIT

In my experience, the fastest way to get the best results with changing habits is to focus on your most important habit first. That's why we spent so much time earlier identifying, prioritizing, analyzing and forecasting habits.

Let's just assume that it actually does take 60 days to create a new habit. And let's assume that about 60 days later, you'll start to lose focus and let that habit slip unless you create more self-awareness and keep on working through any plateaus or barriers you come up against. And, let's assume that you're human, so you'll probably spend another 60 days not working on your habits at all because unexpected things just tend to happen in life. When you add all that up, what you see is that it really takes the average person about half a year to create a new, lifelong habit. Maybe you're way above average, and maybe you're below average, but let's just go with that figure for right now.

If this is true, that means you only really have room in your life to create two new major lifelong habits a year. And I don't know about you, but personally I'm not very good at planning things out any longer than a year from now. Heck, even planning out a daily habit schedule six months from now seems like way too much work for me.

For me, what it really boils down to is that I've only got room for creating and sustaining one new habit in the next few months. That's my focus – creating one new habit and sticking to it for the next 3-6 months.

I think some people tend to go overboard with habit change. We try to change our diet, our workout plan, our work schedule, our sleep schedules, our dating life, our relationship with our family, our spirituality, and our personal hygiene all at once. I don't know about you, but all that sounds overwhelming to me! And it's not very practical, either. If you're like most people, you've probably only got room for one new habit right now.

So if you've only really got room for one new habit right now, which one should it be?

You should focus on your most important habit first and foremost.

If earning more money is your biggest priority right now, focus on creating a new habit that will help you do that. If having a better relationship with your family is the most important priority for you right now, create a new habit that will help you do that. If increasing your spiritual knowledge is your biggest priority right now, focus on creating a new habit that will help you do that. The key here is focus!

It's a bit corny, but I think the acronym for FOCUS (Follow One Course Until Successful) is a great way to remember the importance of focusing on creating one new habit. Don't fall into the trap of trying to change everything at once, because it usually doesn't work, and it tends to end with more feelings of guilt, shame, anger, and depression.

Instead, find an area of life that is really, really important to you right now, and create a new habit that will help you feel more fulfilled and experience more success in that area of your life.

It's really just that simple.

And remember the Snowball Effect we talked about earlier? It applies to habit change, too. When you create a new habit that helps you have a more successful career, it tends to improve your relationships, emotions, spirituality and other areas of life. Humans are holistic. That means that everything in our life affects everything else. When we improve one area of our life, it often helps improve other areas of our life.

If you're behind on your bills, chances are you better get a health checkup in addition to a financial checkup. Why? Because if you haven't been paying attention to your finances, chances are you haven't been paying attention to your health either. While this principle operates in the negative for most people, you can begin to use it to your advantage.

When you create one new habit that will help you fulfill your biggest priority right now, it will automatically help you achieve more goals in other areas of life as well. Why? Because as your awareness in one area of life grows, your awareness of every area of life grows. When you begin to notice all your bad financial habits and improve them, you'll begin to see how similar emotions and bad habits are damaging your health and relationships, too. Most of what we do in life follows a pattern. *When you discover how to fix that bad financial habit you've fallen into, chances are you'll learn how to fix those similar bad habits in your relationships, health, emotions, spirituality, and other key areas of your life.*

LESS IS MORE

When it comes to creating new habits and projects, sometimes less is more. It's better to focus on changing one major habit and succeeding than trying to change everything at once and failing. The more you focus on changing one habit and creating one new habit, the easier it will be to make that change stick. *That's why it's so important to start with your most important habit first.*

MORE TIPS FOR CREATING LASTING HABIT CHANGE AND EMPOWERING HABITS

START EARLY

What do you do first thing in the morning when you wake up? If you're like most people, you probably just follow the same old routine you've been doing for years. It's become habitual.

The problem with unconsciously repeating old habits day in and day out is that they may no longer be supporting your current goals. Let's face it: you're a different person today than you were ten years ago, five years ago, or just one year ago. But being a different person with the same old habits won't get you where you want to go.

You've got to change some of those old habits and instill new habits that will help you achieve your goals and dreams.

One of the best places to start when it comes to changing habits is in your early morning routine. What you do in the morning sets the pace for the rest of the day.

If you feel like you just don't have time to start a new habit right now, try setting your alarm clock half an hour earlier and begin your new habit as soon as you wake up. This can be a great way to start your new workout habit or create a new habit of meditation or another important activity that you can begin by yourself early in the morning.

SAYING NO

If your schedule is already full and you don't feel like you are spending enough time on your biggest priorities, that means you have allowed low priority tasks to fill up your calendar. If that sounds familiar, the best course of action is to start saying no and canceling your commitments to tasks that are no longer serving your best interests.

On any given week, you probably get several requests to spend your time on activities that aren't at the top of your priorities list. That's okay. That's normal. And the best response you can make is to just say no. When you say no to a low-priority task or commitment, it creates room for you to say yes to your highest priorities.

NOTE: We're talking about *your* priorities here, not society's definition of priority or what your parents think should be your priorities. If your highest priority is working on your business, for example, and you turn down the opportunity to serve on a local charity fundraiser committee in order to spend more time working on your business, that's a good choice for you. Your charity-focused friends may think you're selfish, but that's simply their perspective. If your highest priority and best use of time is growing your business, eventually you'll be able to give far more to charity in the long run.

If something is your top priority, it means you need to protect your time and focus on it. Allowing low priority tasks to eat up your time doesn't serve you or anyone else. Spending more time on charity may seem like the good thing to do at the time, but in the long run it's actually worse for you and everyone in your community *if it's not your highest priority activity. If you can, never sacrifice a high priority need in your life in order to fulfill a low priority need.*

When you're working on your highest priority activity, chances are you will be helping the most people the best you can. But in order to do that, you must learn to say no to anything that will get in your way.

If you say yes to everything everyone asks you to do, you'll spend all your time working on everyone else's priorities. But that's not the way to improve your life. The fastest way to improve your life is to work on your highest priority. Working on something less than your highest priority will get you less results.

WHAT TO DO ABOUT ADDICTIVE HABITS YOU CAN'T SEEM TO CHANGE

DISCLAIMER:

I am not a medical or psychological expert and can't give you health or professional advice. If you have a serious addiction, I recommend seeing a medical or psychological professional to help you.

What do you do if you've tried and tried and just can't seem to break a bad habit that's been plaguing you for years?

Here, I'll share my personal experience as a way to show you what worked for me and what might work for you to end even the most difficult bad habits for good.

I used to be incredibly addicted to playing video games. Some days, I could literally spend the entire day from waking up to going to sleep playing video games, with only small breaks in between to eat, drink and go to the bathroom. It was definitely not a healthy habit, and I tried to quit cold turkey several times with no success. A few days, weeks or months later, I'd be back at it playing video games for hours at a time. This habit repeated itself over and over, for several years, and it started to become a major problem for me.

When I began to study psychology and personal development even more, I realized that this habit existed because it was fulfilling a crucial need and purpose in my life.

When you have a bad habit you can't seem to break, ask yourself these questions:

> How is this habit helping me or supporting me?
> What need or needs is this habit fulfilling in my life?
> If I stopped doing this habit completely, what would be missing from my life?

When I started to ask these questions, I realized that playing video games was fun. Pretty obvious, right? But having fun is a very important aspect of life that most of us need and crave. So, I realized that if I wanted to get rid of this habit, I had to replace it with something fun.

After spending more time becoming self-aware and analyzing my habit, I realized that it was also a great solitary activity. As an introvert, I can't spend too much time in social activities or I end up getting drained and tired. So whenever I tried to just go out more with friends, it worked temporarily, but then I would crash, need to spend some time alone, and start back at the video game habit again.

That's how I realized that I needed to replace this bad habit with another habit that I could do by myself, not a social habit.

Finally, I realized that playing video games was also a way for me to relax. It would take my mind off everyday worries and stresses, and help me escape into a more relaxing zone where I could just focus on playing and having fun.

In summary, my addictive habit of playing video games helped add more fun to my life, was a key solitary activity I could fall back on when I felt like being alone, and was a way for me to relax and unwind.

Can you now begin to see why this habit was so addictive for me? Anytime you have a habit that fulfills multiple important functions or roles in your life, it's going to be hard to fix unless you replace it with other habits that help fulfill those key functions and roles.

With that in mind, I realized I needed to create one or several new habits that would help me 1) have more fun while 2) being alone and 3) allow me to relax, unwind and de-stress.

Once I realized that, it was really easy to find some alternative habits. All I did was lock myself in my room, turn of my cell phone and any distractions, grab a notebook and pen and started brainstorming activities I could do that would fulfill one or more of those needs.

Here are some examples:

➢ Walking
➢ Hiking
➢ Running
➢ Taking naps
➢ Getting a massage or bodywork
➢ Exploring a new place or part of town on my own
➢ Reading
➢ Brainstorming new ideas, things to do, business plans and projects

Once I had my list of ideas, it became a lot easier to create some new habits and eliminate my habit of playing video games entirely.

There are a few key takeaways that you should learn from my example.

First of all, *understand the underlying needs and roles your habit fulfills.* Without this awareness, you'll get angry, upset, depressed, and frustrated when you try to change your habit and ultimately fail. The reason you keep failing is because your habit provides important benefits for your life that you need to find another way to replace.

Second, *don't try to replace a habit with a non-complimentary habit.* For example, as an introvert, I couldn't simply hang out with friends and go to more social events to replace my video game habit, because I needed a complimentary habit that I could do alone.

If you're an extrovert, and you find yourself getting addicted to smoking or drinking at social events, you could start reaching out to new social circles where people don't smoke or drink to help get rid of that addiction. Staying home more probably wouldn't be a good solution for an extrovert. This is why self-awareness is so important, and is the ultimate key to lasting habit change.

Third, *difficult habits become easier to change when you have multiple substitute habits or behaviors to compensate.* If I only had hiking on my list of substitute habits for playing video games, I would be very limited in my options. If I sprained an ankle, for example, and couldn't go hiking, I would likely fall back into the habit of video games quickly because I wouldn't be able to go hiking to fulfill my need for fun and relaxation. *Don't limit yourself to only one or two substitutes for a bad habit. The more options you have, the more likely your changes of success in creating lasting habit change.* If you have to invest an hour or more in brainstorming ideas and getting creative, it'll be one of the best investments of time you can make.

CREATING ACCOUNTABILITY AND GETTING THE SUPPORT OF OTHERS

Another great way to help with habit change is to enlist the support of others. Alcoholics Anonymous has helped millions of people quit their addiction to alcohol by using group support, accountability and spirituality to help people heal emotional wounds, make better decisions and change old habits.

You don't have to suffer from a serious addiction to benefit from accountability and group support. Whether you want to start exercising more, eat a healthier diet, or spend more time working on a new project, accountability and group support can be a huge motivator and helpful asset to get your new habit on track.

Today with social media, forums, online groups and sites like MeetUp.com, it's easier than ever to find a group of people like you who can help keep you accountable and encourage you to keep making positive progress. If you're feeling stuck, don't know what group to turn to, and just want some support and to connect with others who are also trying to create positive changes in their lives, come join our free group on Facebook and let's help each other create some better habits. You can join us at:

www.facebook.com/groups/
EntrepreneurSuccessGroup

MODEL AND ASSOCIATE WITH SUCCESSFUL PEOPLE

Who do you hang out with and how do they affect you?

The people we spend time with end up creating a gradual, but steady pull on us in the direction they're heading. If you hang out with people who drink a lot, chances are you'll drink more. If you hang out with people who go to the opera every week, chances are you'll spend more time at the opera. It sounds obvious, but most of us don't spend enough time working on cultivating relationships that support us and help us move in the right direction.

We also tend to compare ourselves, consciously and subconsciously, to the people we spend time with. Who do you compare yourself to? If you compare yourself to unproductive people, you might feel like you're incredibly productive and successful. But if you compare yourself to a super-productive multimillionaire, you might feel lazy and unproductive in comparison. It's all relative. Your peer group will determine, in many cases, how you see yourself, who you consciously and unconsciously compare yourself to, and what progress you do or do not make as a result.

If you have want to start a habit of running a marathon, for example, and none of your friends can even run a mile, it's going to make that habit even harder to form. You'll probably have to step out and meet new people – other runners who you can train with, learn from, and hold you accountable to your goals.

When you're trying to make changes in any area of your life, look to see who you know who is on a similar path already and try to spend more time with them. If you don't know anyone who would be a good fit, then reach out and try to meet new people who are on the same path. Life's too short to travel alone or with the wrong companions.

If you want to move up and achieve new and bigger goals, surround yourself with others who are doing the same or who have already achieved what you want to achieve. It'll make your journey a lot easier, and a lot more fun and fulfilling.

KEEP MAKING PROGRESS

It's impossible to make consistent progress in the right direction without awareness. If you're aware, you won't let bad habits rob your health, steal your success, and destroy your most precious relationships. That's why we started this journey with the Time Tracking Exercise because when you do it right, you can't trick yourself anymore. The numbers don't lie. When you start to pay attention to how you're actually spending your time, you can't hide your bad habits anymore. You can't hide the truth once you've seen it.

For those of you who are really inspired, you can use the same six step process in this book to improve any and every area of your life. In addition to the Time Tracking Exercise, you can use a similar exercise to track other key areas of your life. You can track your expenses and how they're impacting your finances. You can track your diet and exercise habits to determine how they're impacting your health. You can track your social interactions to determine how they're impacting your social life and relationships.

Whenever you do something that increases your awareness, you will begin to improve your life. If this book has helped you increase your awareness of how you spend your time, then I've done my job.

Now it's your turn to use that new awareness to create a new habit and change your life forever.

Here's to your success!

SPECIAL FACEBOOK GROUP

Come join our Facebook group just for readers like you who want to improve their life and live at the highest levels of success, happiness and fulfillment. In this group we'll be sharing our successes and support with each other so that we can all continue to grow together.

Come join us here on Facebook:

www.facebook.com/groups/
EntrepreneurSuccessGroup

FREE BLOGGING FOR BUSINESS TRAINING

If you're a business owner and want to learn how to start a blog for your business that makes a profit, I've developed a free online training program to teach you everything from how to build your blog to getting traffic to monetizing it.

You can get the free training at:

www.BlogBusinessSchool.com

WANT TO
LEARN MORE?

Come study with Tom Corson-Knowles in his 5-star online educational courses for entrepreneurs, authors, artists, creative people and anyone who wants to learn how to live the life of their dreams. Tom is one of the top instructors at Udemy with over 27,000 students and 200+ 5-star reviews.

As a special "thank you" for reading this book, you can get access to all of Tom's courses for 25% to 50% off the regular price with the special links below:

UNLEASH YOUR CREATIVE GENIUS

https://www.udemy.com/unleash-your-creative-genius/?couponCode=TCKBooks

BUILD YOUR OWN CUSTOM WORDPRESS WEBSITE AND BLOG IN A DAY

https://www.udemy.com/how-to-create-a-website/?couponCode=TCKBooks

EMAIL MARKETING MADE EASY

https://www.udemy.com/email-marketing-secrets/?couponCode=TCKBooks

HOW TO WRITE A NONFICTION BOOK THAT ACTUALLY SELLS

https://www.udemy.com/how-to-write-a-nonfiction-book-that-actually-sells/?couponCode=TCKBooks

HOW TO BECOME A BESTSELLING AUTHOR ON AMAZON KINDLE

https://www.udemy.com/kindle-publishing-course/?couponCode=TCKBooks

SYSTEMIZE, AUTOMATE, DELEGATE YOUR BUSINESS TO SUCCESS

https://www.udemy.com/systemize-automate-delegate/?couponCode=TCKBooks

CONNECT WITH TOM

Thank you so much for taking the time to read this book. I'm excited for you to start your path to creating the life of your dreams.

If you have any questions of any kind, feel free to contact me at:

www.tckpublishing.com/contact

You can follow me on Twitter:

http://www.twitter.com/juicetom

And connect with me on Facebook:

www.tckpublishing.com/facebook

You can check out my publishing blog for the latest updates here:

www.tckpublishing.com/

I'm wishing you the best of health, happiness and success!

Here's to you!

Tom Corson-Knowles

ABOUT THE AUTHOR

TOM CORSON-KNOWLES is the #1 Amazon best-selling author of *The Kindle Publishing Bible* and *How To Make Money With Twitter*, among others. He lives in Kapaa, Hawaii. Tom loves educating and inspiring other entrepreneurs to succeed and live their dreams.

Learn more at:

Http://amazon.com/author/business

Get the free Kindle publishing and marketing video training series from Tom at:

http://www.ebookpublishingschool.com

OTHER BOOKS BY
TOM CORSON-KNOWLES

Destroy Your Distractions

Email Marketing Mastery

The Book Marketing Bible: 39 Proven Ways to Build Your Author Platform and Promote Your Books on a Budget

Schedule Your Success: How to Master the One Key Habit That Will Transform Every Area of Your Life

You Can't Cheat Success!: How The Little Things You Think Aren't Important Are The Most Important of All

Guest Blogging Goldmine

Rules of the Rich: 28 Proven Strategies for Creating a Healthy, Wealthy and Happy Life and Escaping the Rat Race Once and for All

Systemize, Automate, Delegate: How to Grow a Business While Traveling, on Vacation and Taking Time Off

The Kindle Publishing Bible: How To Sell More Kindle ebooks On Amazon

The Kindle Writing Bible: How To Write a Bestselling Nonfiction Book From Start To Finish

The Kindle Formatting Bible: How To Format Your Ebook For Kindle Using Microsoft Word

How To Make Money With Twitter

101 Ways To Start A Business For Less Than $1,000

Facebook For Business Owners: Facebook Marketing For Fan Page Owners and Small Businesses

How To Reduce Your Debt Overnight: A Simple System To Eliminate Credit Card And Consumer Debt

The Network Marketing Manual: Work From Home And Get Rich In Direct Sales

Dr. Corson's Top 5 Nutrition Tips

The Vertical Gardening Guidebook: How To Create Beautiful Vertical Gardens, Container Gardens and Aeroponic Vertical Tower Gardens at Home

ONE LAST THING...

Thanks for reading! If you enjoyed this book or found it useful I'd be very grateful if you'd post a short review on Amazon. Your support really does make a difference and I read all the reviews personally so I can get your feedback and make this book even better.

Thanks again for your support!